The
Way

The Way

From Darkness to Light

Jannah A. Mitchell

iUniverse

THE WAY
FROM DARKNESS TO LIGHT

iUniverse books may be ordered through booksellers or by contacting:

iUniverse
1663 Liberty Drive
Bloomington, IN 47403
www.iuniverse.com
1-800-Authors (1-800-288-4677)

Because of the dynamic nature of the Internet, any web addresses or links contained in this book may have changed since publication and may no longer be valid. The views expressed in this work are solely those of the author and do not necessarily reflect the views of the publisher, and the publisher hereby disclaims any responsibility for them.

Any people depicted in stock imagery provided by Thinkstock are models, and such images are being used for illustrative purposes only. Certain stock imagery © Thinkstock.

ISBN: 978-1-4917-5604-1 (sc)
ISBN: 978-1-4917-5603-4 (e)

Library of Congress Control Number: 2015900232

Printed in the United States of America.

iUniverse rev. date: 1/14/2015

www.stillwaterspublishing8@gmail.com

Dedication

This book is dedicated to Almighty God, who inspired it and commissioned it. Father I give you all the glory.

This book is dedicated to all who are searching for answers...

Contents

Acknowledgments

I would like to thank my daughter, Angel and my sister, Mary Ann for assisting me by reading this book before publishing. Their encouraging words gave me the courage to complete the publishing process.

There is a way that seemeth
right to a man, but the
end thereof is death…..
(Proverbs 16:25 King James Version)

Introduction

Man is born searching. From the moment our heads emerge into earth's atmosphere; we are searching. If you ask any man or woman exactly what they are seeking, they may or may not be able to share the object of their personal quest. Some can name it, and some cannot.

I believe that every man and woman born is searching for the same thing. Though they may call it by various names and define it in different ways, -- there is but one ultimate goal.

One person might call it *love*. Another might call it *peace*. Another might say I'm searching for my *purpose in life*. There's a group that calls it *Nirvana*. Another group calls it *enlightenment*. Some call it *self-realization*. Some call it *truth*. A few call it *meaning*. Many even venture to call it *God*... Whatever the descriptor, and the list is endless -- I posit that they are all looking for, searching for, longing for, yearning for the same ultimate goal.

This book is inspired by Almighty God to provide some guidance in what is often a life-long, endless, and unfulfilled search.

I claim no personal expertise. This wisdom has been available for mankind for thousands of years. My pen has responded to the inspiration of the Creator. I am qualified to speak on this matter, because I am a fellow-human being with comparable human experiences. I searched aim-lessly until I was led to *The Way*.

I have been a member of Living Word Christian Center since 2000. I graduated from the School of Ministry at Living Word in June 2002. I served in the Pastoral Care Ministry and the Prayer Ministry for many years. I travelled with missions teams to various parts of the world including: Bogota and Cali, Colombia; Hyderabad, India; Panama City, Panama; and Port-au-Prince and Carrefour, Haiti. I ministered in churches, orphanages, feeding centers, pris-ons, and schools in those areas. In prior years I tutored and ministered to prisoners in the Cook County Jail in Chicago, Illinois.

I am a recent retiree. I feel that my life's work is to introduce men and women to Jesus Christ. A crucial part of that assignment is follow-up teaching for new Christians, to establish a firm foundation for Christian living. Saints need to understand and benefit from their covenant with

Almighty God. Heaven is not limited to the outer reaches of space. Heaven can be experienced right here on earth. I am dedicated to inspiring deeper understanding of God's plan, according to His Word in the Holy Bible.

The reading of this book requires a deep desire to know and understand. Its study requires a sincere heart and an open mind -- a willingness to admit that the search heretofore has not proved fruitful. This book requires faith that there is power in the universe to bring to the seeker that for which he sincerely seeks. Realize that the answers to your questions may not line up with your favored paradigm for life, your current religious beliefs, nor your favorite philosophies. Dare to allow for corrections. Isn't it worth it to find and embark upon *The Way*? Isn't it worth it to find all that you have been searching for?

I have included scriptures from the Bible. They are identified by *italics*. I encourage you to read each one aloud. The Bible location of each scripture is indicated so that you can look it up in your own Bible. The Word of God is so powerful that the mere reading of a passage **aloud** can change your circumstances.

I pray that God blesses you to hold on to this book once you acquire it, and to read it cover to cover. I pray that the mind of every reader is divinely changed and enlightened by the contact. I pray that this book causes revelation knowledge to flow in the life of each reader who seeks and finds *The Way* in its pages… I decree that God's anointing flows as you turn each page. In Jesus' Name. Amen.

Chapter One

My Way or the Highway

In the United States of America, citizens often pride themselves on being autonomous and independent. The anthem is, "I did it my way!" They think: "My way is unique. My way is different. My way is best. I am not open to your way or his way or the way that they are taking. MY WAY RULES. I know it all. None of my ideas can be challenged. If they are, I will defend them to the death -- whether they are right or wrong. I just want to do it my way, because I have the freedom to do so. I am comfortable with my ideas and my opinions and my way of thinking, and I don't want to change. I am special. I value being different from them (whoever *them* happens to be). I took two semesters of psychology and one course in sociology in junior college, so I am an expert on most issues. I have a Ph.D. in Urban Studies, so I know how this thing goes.

Advice is neither required nor appreciated. My ideology is supreme, and it's right. The paradigm that shapes my life, the lens through which I view the world, is the correct one…"

I believe it was Socrates who said: "The unexamined life is not worth living." I agree. I have learned, over the last 50 years that we need to examine our lives periodically. We need to objectively evaluate our beliefs and theories on a regular basis. Critical analysis requires an open mind and a willingness to be occasionally what is most dreaded by human beings -- *wrong*! Too many of us wait until some tragic occurrence or some life-altering experience. Insurmountable obstacles then force us to look at the quality of our belief systems and to measure how far those belief systems have gotten us. Too many of us require forced examination *vs.* regular self-examination of our subconscious driving forces.

Man tends to depend on his catalogue of experiences, what *experts* have told him, what authorities say in textbooks, on television messages, and on internet content.

I challenge you to lay aside your way for a few hours. I challenge you to be open to the possibility that some of your basic assumptions are erroneous. I challenge you to read this book with your inner being, your spirit, and not just with your eyes. Allow for the possibility that God has brought this book to you, so that He can give you the desires of your heart -- the very object of your lifelong search, whatever you have named it. Believe in a miracle for your life.

Chapter Two

How to Begin to See

Now Looking and Projection

The beginning is at the end. The place to begin is where you have ended up -- where you stand right now.

After all, your thoughts, beliefs, assumptions, knowledge, education, and life experiences have landed you right here...right now, with this book in your hands. This situation is no coincidence.

Ask yourself: Am I in a "good" place? Is this where I was planning to go? Have I reached the goals I set for myself? Do I even remember those goals? Have I realized my dream? Do I even remember my original dream? Is my presence making the world better? Am I helping humanity? Is my presence making the world worse? Am I hindering mankind?

If your answer is *no* to any of the first eight

questions, then you need to consider your ways. If you evaluate your life as making the world worse or you see yourself as a hindrance to mankind, you are in an emergency state! Don't put this book down until you have at least one clue to your redemption.

Why? -- because your way is not working to bring you to your desired state. Your way has failed. Unfortunately, even some of my Christian readers may find that they are falling short. Be not dismayed. There are answers for you here.

By objectively looking at now, what I call *now-looking*, you can determine if you need a course correction. A fruitful extension to *now-looking* is *projection* -- an imaginary projection of today's mindsets, philosophies, habits and activities twenty years into the future. Will beautiful panoramic scenarios manifest from a continuation of current thoughts and activity? Or will some catastrophic monstrosity be birthed to darken your future landscapes? Although I do not elaborate further about *now-looking* and *projection*, they are valuable tools if you take the time to use them.

For example, you're a smoker. All medical science, your significant other, documentaries on television, and even your mother have urged you to quit smoking to save your health. But you, in your infinite wisdom, are determined to live life your way -- regardless of the consequences. Extend that stubborn, unhealthy behavior twenty years into the future. See yourself in a hospital bed, with an oxygen tank that follows you everywhere you go, dried up and miserable. You lay there dying in front of medical science, your significant other, all the information you got from documentaries on T.V. and even your mother. Would it really be worth it just to prove that you are an individual? Would it really be worth it for your last breath to breathe out, "I did it my way!!" The problem here is not so much smoking as it is captivity by the *my way syndrome*.

Smoking is an easily-accessible example of *now-looking* and *projection*. I ask you to apply *now-looking* and *projection* to the future of your eternal spirit. In that arena, the stakes become much higher.

If after a little *now-looking* and *projection* you are convinced that it's time for consideration and examination of your life, you're in the right book at the right time. God has heard your secret cries for help, and He has provided assistance -- probably in a way you never expected.

The My Way Syndrome

Throughout this book, I will mention *the my way syndrome*. This syndrome is a form of stronghold -- a powerful thought pattern rooted in error, that stands against the Truth of God's Word. The *my way syndrome* blocks the gate to knowledge and wisdom. It sets itself up as the only truth and allows entry to no opposing thought. This syndrome begins with childhood input to the subconscious mind of a person. At that time, there is little power of discrimination or reasoning ability available. The lessons learned early from authority figures (parents, teachers, television) and experiences become the basis for the person's *Truth*. Later, these accepted conclusions become such an adamant conglomeration of preconceived ideas, that they are nearly impenetrable to new and different information. The subconscious mind resists anything other than what it has collected and put together as *my way*.

People argue, fight, and even kill each other to protect that stronghold of "knowledge" -- no matter how erroneous it may be. It is defended as if its loss will cause physical death.

The minds of some readers will revolt at the thought of walking a standard path in life. A rebellious chord within them will try to pull them out of this book. Subconsciously they think, "This book threatens *my way*."

The *my way syndrome* is a firmly established modern paradigm. I can't blame it on Frank

Sinatra's song alone, although the song is compelling. I believe it has to do with the rebellion of the human psyche against sameness. Everyone wants to choose how and what he or she will be -- often at grave risk to life and limb. If one decides to be a part of a group, he/she wants to select the characteristics of the group to which he/she will pledge allegiance and admit connection.

Were I a more profound thinker, I could probably trace the source of this aversion to sameness. Let it suffice to say that such mindsets are part of the modern world system to which many world citizens subscribe. Biblically, God supports mankind's free will and choice.

A Choice

> *See I have set before thee this day life and good, and death and evil;...*
> *I call heaven and earth to record this day against you, that I have set before you life and death, blessing and cursing: therefore choose life, that both thou and thy seed may live:...*
> (Deut. 30:15, 19 KJV)

In the passage above God is giving the Israelites an opportunity to determine their futures. Today the options have not changed.

The Way has not changed. The results of each decision have not changed.

We must choose. However, success, true happiness, joy, peace, and eternal life only come from the right selection. The correct choice is easily identified by its agreement with God's Word (the Holy Bible). All of life's answers are in that Book -- the Holy Bible.

Some of you are ready to close this book now, as you mouth expletives against the very thought of Christianity. Trust me when I say that the real you, the spiritual being sitting inside your earthen body, wants you to keep reading. The inner you, that inward man, wants to continue. (Rom. 7:22; Eph. 3:16 KJV)

Listen, I know you've tried everything else -- and none of it worked. I know because I did too. I was a student of world religions -- Buddhism, Islam, theosophy, philosophy, New Age, history, and psychology. I even followed a guru for awhile. I have worshipped at the feet of higher education. I read Carl Jung, Sigmund Freud, Herodotus, Aristotle, Plato, Philo Judaeus, and many other church fathers, historians, philosophers, and psychologists. I have read extensively -- Egyptian religion, the Book of the Dead, the apocrypha, The Book of Enoch, numerous occult writings that promised light on the path. I searched for the golden fleece, the holy grail, and the philosopher's stone -- for the answer. But I found none.

I found none until I was willing to open my heart and my mind to the possibility that I'd been searching for love…and truth and enlightenment in all the wrong places. I had to admit that perhaps the answer was right in front of my eyes all the time. That takes courage. In the Name of Jesus, I *en-courage* you to stick with this book and find your answer.

Chapter Three

A Working Definition of The Way

Webster Definitions

In this book, I refer to the *way* and/or *path*. I also mention *highway*. All three terms are used in the Bible. All three terms refer to an established place for passage, travel, or a journey. All refer to a course that may be followed to a desired destination.

Webster defines *way: Literally, a passing; hence a passage; the place of passing; hence a road of any kind; a highway; a private road; a lane; a street; any place for the passing of men, cattle, or other animals; **a word of very comprehensive signification**.* Other definitions include: *length of space; direction or motion of travel; regular course; manner of doing any thing; method; scheme of management; manner of thinking or behavior; method; manner of practice;*

11

method or plan of life. (Webster, Noah, *American Dictionary of the English Language.* Willard, OH: Donnelley, 2006.)

Webster defines *way* as *(1) direction of motion, progress, facing, pointing, etc; route; line of tendency of action; (2) that along which one passes or progresses to reach some place; the track a person or thing travels or has traveled in his or its progress or passage; a course from one place to another; a passage, road, street, track, or path of any kind.* Other definitions included: *journey; manner; method; mode; fashion; style, as the way of expressing one's ideas; habitual method of life or action; occupation; calling; determined course; resolved mode of action or conduct.* (*The Webster International Dictionary.* London, England: G. & C. Merriam Company, 1909)

Webster defines a *path* as: *a way trodden by the feet of man or beast; applied to the ground only and never to a paved street in the city; any narrow way beaten by foot; precept, rules prescribed; course of life; a moral government.* (Webster, *American Dictionary*, 2006)

Webster defines *path* as: *a trodden or beaten way; a track made (usually) incidentally by foot travel; a narrow more or less finished way across country, up a mountain, etc.; a footway; a walk as in a garden; more generally any way or road; a specifically constructed track for racing; a way, course, or track, in which anything moves or has moved; a route; passage;*

an established way. Also a course or way of life, con-duct, thought, reasoning, etc. (*Webster International Dictionary* 1909)

Webster defines *highway* as: *a public road; a way open to all passengers; so called either because it is a great or public road, or because the earth has raised to form a dry path; course, road, train of action.* (*Webster International Dictionary* 1909)

Highway is defined by Webster as: *a main road or thoroughfare, hence a road or way open to the use of the public, including in the broadest sense of the term ways upon water as well as upon land. Originally highways designated a chief or principle way, which being traveled by the public in general, was, early in English history, brought under the protection of the king's peace; and highway in this sense is distin-guished from byway or bypath.* (*Webster International Dictionary* 1909)

A byway or bypath is defined as a secluded, pri-vate, or obscure way; a side path or road. (*Webster International Dictionary* 1909)

Wow, that's a lot of definition for such a lit-tle, three-letter word, *way*. As Webster so aptly noted, *way* is **a word of very comprehensive sig-nification**. (Webster, *American Dictionary* 2006) Its meanings are multiple and cover physical, mental, and spiritual territories. I felt it a duty to present all these definitions and identify those which will apply for this book. They are all relevant, but everything cannot be explored in one volume. I desire to focus the reader's attention by giving the definition of *way* I used for the scope of this volume.

The astute reader will see applications for other definitions of the word as we journey on *The Way*. Count it as revelation from Almighty God!

Did I say "journey on *The Way*"? Yes, I did. If you have made it this far; if you waded through those definitions and are anticipating the refined definition to be used in this book -- then you are already beginning a life-changing journey. I pause and pray that Almighty God, in His infinite love and mercy, will bless you with answers, direction, and the very desires of your heart as you read on…

Our Working Definitions

In this book we will use the following definitions for way: (1) manner and content of thinking; (2) method or plan of life; (3) calling; and (4) direction of travel.

You might say that's still a lot of definition. These simplified definitions roll together.
The manner and content of your thinking determines your methods/plan of life and conduct -- as well as your perceived "calling" in

life. What and how you think determines the direction you travel in life.

The Bible puts it simply in Proverbs:

> *For as he thinketh in his heart, so is he;…* (Prov. 23:7 KJV)

The next logical questions are, "What should I think?" and "Can man even control the content of his thoughts? Isn't that just automatic?"

Birds of a Feather

These questions we will answer as we proceed. Let it suffice to say now: Everything you do was first a thought. Where did the thought originate? It probably originated in the mass of subconscious material we discussed earlier, which supports the *my way syndrome*. That mass of beliefs drives your actions, and even attracts similar thinkers of such thoughts to you. So if the convictions of your subconscious mind are extremely erroneous, they attract and hold additional error like a mind magnet in a sci-fi movie.

That's just the way the mind works. Consider thoughts as birds, and then remember the old adage, "Birds of a feather flock together." Don't your closest friends and acquaintances think pretty much like you? Not your family!

Family never gets it. I'm talking about those people you prefer to be around, those people who "understand" what's going on, and they "understand" you. If you are a skin-head racist who supports only the Aryan race, do you hang out with friends who travel around the world in the Peace Corps to bring humanitarian aid to the poor and needy? I think not. Are you more likely to be a Red Cross volunteer or a cross-burning Ku Klux Klan member? Let's be for real here! Let's be honest! To the natural (non-spiritual) mind this phenomenon may seem to be physical, external attraction, but it's thought-driven. *Birds of a feather...*

[**Note to the reader:** I am not targeting skin-heads or racists. This example is used to make my point about how associations tend to support one's beliefs. Although I do not advocate the ideologies of racists, I must stand on their side for a moment. These persons were not born hating anyone. They were once sweet, innocent babies just as we all were. They were taught their beliefs in the same way we all were taught our individual and collective beliefs. Praise God, none of us can be blamed for our erroneous thinking, but we must accept blame for not making efforts to change once we've heard the Truth and know *The Way*. How many of you are spittin' mad right now? Good! At least I got a rise out of you. Let's go on.]

Some of you may be ready to put this book down, so you can say -- "Well, I didn't finish the book and I don't know *The Way*. Therefore, I can't be held responsible for knowing." My friend, if this book has come into your hands, it is your opportunity to learn, to understand, and to change. If you do not take advantage of the opportunity, you still have no excuse. What are you going to say in the end, "Well, Lord that Jannah made me angry so I couldn't correct my course." What's more important friend -- your vanity or your life?

Chapter Four

The Timeless Path

Lost

Have you ever been lost? Did you know you were lost as soon as you made that wrong turn or got on the wrong train or bus? Or did you travel for another 15, 20, 30 minutes -- or maybe even an hour before admitting, "I'm lost." Did you ever admit you were lost?

If you are a driver or even a public transportation passenger; if you are a bike rider or a walker; I know you have been lost at least once. The likelihood of getting lost increases when you're seeking a destination you have never travelled to before, or you're approaching a familiar destination from a completely new direction.

Some women say it's a *man thing* -- that men don't ever want to admit that they are lost. I think it's a human thing. Anyone, male or female, can be lost -- and may deny it until it looks hopeless. At that point, saving face is no longer an issue of concern. That person simply wants to find his/her way. Being lost can be very scary.

That's why finding *The Way* is important. Being lost is uncomfortable and scary. However, due to the *my way syndrome*, many will not admit that they are lost until they are in a hopeless, dead end circumstance. At the dead end, or brick wall as I've always called it -- there seems to be no way out. All progress or motion ceases. The traveler just stands and stares at the dead end sign or the brick wall, and the sign or the wall stares back. The traveler panics and asks him- or herself, "Where do I go from here? Fine mess I've gotten myself into."

Perhaps ahead is a dark forest with creepy sounds and the potential for really getting lost. Even though it is not a brick wall, it is still foreboding. The traveler realizes that walking into the forest would not be a good idea. His troubles could increase exponentially in the twisting pathways of that darker unfamiliar place. Visions of being devoured by creatures unknown to man dance in the traveler's head and wreak havoc on his/her emotions. Not a pleasant place to be!

No one seeks to be lost, not intentionally. It may appear that a person does so because the person continuously makes poor choices. These poor decisions are mostly based on ignorance or the *my way syndrome*. The *my way syndrome* leads one to take risks and defy logical behavior, just to prove himself right. No, it doesn't make sense, but it is behind the self-defeating behaviors of many people.

Now, a life traveler can continue down their chosen path to a dead end, a brick wall, or a dark forest. There they can experience the resulting physical, psychological, and emotional terrors. Or a person can read this book and find out how to avoid future pitfalls that have destroyed the lives of many of their family members, friends, and acquaintances.

It doesn't mean you're not a real man or a real woman, or a real hip teenager if you use a roadmap. I'd rather be caught with a roadmap in my hands, than find myself at the end of a dark, lonely road without a clue.

That is how many lives end -- alone, in the dark, lost...

A Clue

I want you to have a clue. I don't want you to be lost. I want you to read and embrace this message, as the life-saving, life-engendering word that it is. It wasn't my idea! I did not create

The Way. I didn't start out knowing about *The Way.* But at some points in my life, I stopped long enough to listen and learn. Various signposts pointed me in the right direction. And now I walk *The Way.*

There are no monetary costs attached to walking *The Way.* I don't get a commission for telling you about it. But the love that God has put into my heart makes it mandatory for me to share the good news with you.

You don't have to be lost and confused. You don't have to have constant feelings of guilt and condemnation. You know that you are not living as you should. You know that you are not treating people the way you should. You don't have to be trapped by mistakes you made as a youth. You don't have to be paralyzed by the wrongs done to you. You can have peace, joy, and happiness right here on earth. You don't have to wait until you die and go to heaven. God has given us a roadmap that circumvents trial and error and takes us directly to the destination we seek.

Finding *The Way* is important because it can improve your life journey. Finding *The Way* and walking it can improve the quality of your life and bring you peace and happiness.

> *Be careful for nothing; but in every thing by prayer and supplication with*

thanksgiving let your requests be made known unto God.

And the peace of God, which passeth all understanding, shall keep your hearts and minds through Christ Jesus. (Phil. 4:6-7 KJV)

Ask God to help you right now. Ask Him to help you read on and understand what you are reading. Ask Him to help you believe His Word. Ask Him for that peace that is so awesome that it is beyond our understanding, but it exists all the same.

Consider Your Ways

Only believe that God loves you and cares about you individually. In Haggai God says to us:

Now therefore thus saith the Lord of hosts; Consider your ways. (Hag.1:5 KJV)

Yes, we each have a way or several ways that we are trying to walk in life. God asks us to consider (think about, think about carefully, evaluate, reflect upon) our way(s).

God then tells us:

*Go up to the mountain, and bring
wood, and build the house; and I will
take pleasure in it, and I will be glori-
fied, saith the Lord.*

*Ye looked for much, and lo it came to
little…* (Hag. 1:8-9a KJV)

God wants us to go up the mountain. A
mountain is a high place from which we can
view all that is around us. A mountain is a place
of greater perspective. Once there, God asks that
we gather building materials. The house God
speaks of in this passage is a physical temple on
earth, His temple.

But in the New Testament we learn that each
person who gives their life to God is a temple.

*What? Know ye not that your body is
the temple of the Holy Ghost which is
in you, which ye have of God, and ye
are not your own?* (1 Cor. 6:19 KJV)

So this Old Testament scripture in Haggai
also speaks to building up the temple that each
of us potentially is. God is pleased and glori-
fied when we take the building materials from
His Word and apply them to our lives. Doing
so puts us on *The Way*. Even as God gives us

the instructions in Haggai, Chapter 1, God adds: *Ye looked for much, and lo it came to little…* (Hag. 1:9 KJV)

At the outset of your journey, you expected a pot of gold sitting at the end of the path -- that pot being filled with whatever you anticipated as your ultimate goal. You looked for much but so far you have found little. How do I know? Because the Bible tells us so, right here in Haggai, as if God already knew the outcome. **There is only one way.** It has been identified and mapped out for us long ago. It never becomes antiquated. It never becomes irrelevant.

How do you react when someone suggests that you are lost? Do you become defensive? Do you become angry? Do you become more determined to dig in and make your way work? Unfortunately, these are three common reactions to any suggestion that you are on the wrong road to your goal; and prevalent reactions to any suggested change.

Some of you might say: "I know some people who have everything -- like the movie stars and rap artists. They have money, fame, cars, mansions, and the mate of their choice." My response: Are they happy? Why are so many of them on drugs, in rehab, participating in life-threatening behaviors, committing suicide? Many of them think they can buy salvation by giving to the poor and needy. Though that behavior is commendable and brings blessing, there is still a need for a personal relationship with God. There is only one way -- *The Way*.

The egocentric nature of the *my way syndrome* makes suggested change appear as an admission of prior error. The ego portion of our minds, the "I" in each of us, does not want to admit to error. It can be someone else's mistake, but not my error. So rather than consider our ways before encountering catastrophe, we muddle on in error until we face the dead end, brick wall, or dark forest.

At the beginning of this book, there is a page with a single quotation from Proverbs.

> *There is a way that seemeth right to a man, but the end thereof is death...* (Prov.16:25 KJV)

The way you take can look right, feel right, and meet with the approval of the masses -- but still lead to death. Many crack addicts and heroine addicts probably tell themselves: "Everybody else I know is doing it. Those who don't smoke crack or snort heroine must be nerds and geeks. I'm in the in crowd. I'm on the cutting edge of what's in vogue!" Many smokers probably stand behind the anthem, "If cigarettes were so bad for you; they wouldn't be legal. I'm not violating any laws like drug addicts. I'm not addicted. I just enjoy smoking. It calms me down."

These examples are used because they are common activities in which many of you have participated or somehow witnessed. I could go on and talk about theft, murder, abortion, lying, cheating, prostituting oneself, deserting one's children, abandoning one's spouse, etc. The list of potential questionable activities is endless.

But often the participants have constructed elaborate defense statements to justify why their actions are o.k. These explanations are part of a *mental stronghold* -- a cohesive group of erroneous thought patterns that direct a person's life and lifestyle. The mental stronghold does not make itself available for review, consideration, or judgment. It requires effort to bring it to the light -- but to the light it must come.

Chapter Five

The Origin of Our Beliefs

Thinking About Our Beliefs

It would be premature to answer the logical follow-up questions identified in Chapter 3 now. As a reminder, the questions were: "What should I think?" and "Can man even control the content of his thoughts? Isn't that just automatic?"

I believe these questions can best be answered by acquiring some background from your life first. To do this, you must be honest with yourself and me. Otherwise, you'll miss the point of the exercise. Use the blank form on the next page to record your responses. Some of you may be ready to stop reading because you don't like *exercises in books*. I don't like them either. But this is the best way to begin answering our questions. And I promise, this is the only exercise.

Think about one of your deepest-held beliefs.

Choose that belief that no one can change -- a belief that could not be removed from your mind with a sledgehammer; a belief that is embedded in the core of your being; a belief that you **KNOW** is right. I am not fishing for a "God statement". This statement doesn't have to include the word "God" in it at all. Your belief may sound like a famous saying/quotation (because it is). **Examples:**

- The Cubs are the best baseball team ever.
- Women with blonde hair have more fun than brunettes.
- Putting chains on your tires is the best way to drive in winter weather.
- Asian Americans are smarter than other Americans and always make good grades.
- All physically-challenged people are nice.
- It's not what you know; it's who you know.
- Some guys have all the luck.
- You can't become addicted to marijuana, and it doesn't harm you.
- All African Americans are lazy and shiftless.
- Drinking a few beers daily doesn't make you an alcoholic.
- One dose of heroin or crack cocaine will not produce addiction.

Before you complete the blank Exercise Form below, read pages 30 - 32. Also review the completed Example Form on page 33. Doing so will give you a better idea of how to answer your questions.

Exercise Form

Belief	
First person(s) who spoke belief	
Three friends or acquaintances who believed the same thing	
Book, teacher, famous person, TV show, or movie that supported the belief	
Actual life experience that verified belief	
Your activities (groups, clubs, org) in which you participate that confirms or supports belief	

Help: Ask yourself: "What statement of truth do I know that covers all women, all men, all children, education, all families, money, success, fear, relationships between the sexes, politics, all politicians, all churches, all ministers, or all Christians...? Choose only one.

Write that belief at the top of the sheet of the blank form. Don't be ashamed. Don't be afraid. You're alone. Though I'm with you via this book, I can't actually see your response.

Some of you may have difficulty identifying a belief. These subtle "nuggets of wisdom" are so well camouflaged in the fabric of your mind that you may not be able to distinguish them from your "personality".

If you've been able to find a statement of belief, do you feel a little reluctant to write down your belief; even though you've held and defended that belief for years and maybe even decades? As you write that belief, does the belief seem a little shakier than it was when it was safely hidden inside your mind? Do you feel uncomfortable revealing that belief to the light of day? Do you want to stop reading and participating right now? Do you feel that this simple exercise may somehow threaten your belief?

I assure you, you are not alone. Core beliefs [deeply-held beliefs] become part of the individual that believes them. They are part of the soul. Therefore, challenging or changing or even looking at that belief may prove "painful" to the believer.

Don't worry. Challenging and changing your beliefs is not my personal assignment. My assignment is to talk to you about *The Way*; to point out *The Way*. It is your decision, and yours alone, to begin walking *The Way*. All challenging, changing, deleting, and replacement of beliefs begins on *The Way* and is accomplished by you and a heavenly team of experts. I'm helping you to understand how you got to your present location. That's the beginning of helping you to go somewhere else. Do you desire to go somewhere else?

O.K. Write your belief next to the word "belief" at the top of the paper. Be honest with me and yourself, realizing that you are not on track to reach the destination you once set for yourself.

NO. You are not a loser. You are a human being with human frailties; subject to deception and seeking guidance. My desire is to help you find *The Way*.

Follow the instructions below to fill in the remaining boxes. Use my example form on page 33 for additional assistance.

Box 1 - Who is the first person you ever heard speak this belief, in the words above (at the top of your page) or similar words?

Box 2 - Name three friends or acquaintances who believe the same thing or have a similar belief

Box 3 - Name a book, teacher, famous person, or movie that supports this belief

Box 4 - Name an actual experience you had that verifies the truth of your belief. No details are required. Just 2-3 words to help you identify the experience.

Box 5 - Name activities, groups, clubs, organizations in which you participate or participated in that confirm or support the belief.

Review the example form on the next page.

Example Completed Form:

BELIEF	*It's not what you know. It's who you know.*
First person who spoke belief	*My father and his friends often talked about getting a job. They would say that if you knew the hiring person, you had a better chance. Whenever someone got a break, they would discuss who that person knew to obtain that benefit.*
Three friends or acquaintances who believed the same thing	*My father, my brother, and some of my male friends echoed the same feelings when they were having hard times*
Book, teacher, famous person, TV show or movie that supported the belief	*I saw a movie about slavery. Most of the slaves were treated badly. One lady got a job in the kitchen instead of the fields. She had been a good friend of the Master's daughter when they were small.*
Actual life experience that verified belief	*I applied to be an airline stewardess. It was for transatlantic flights. I could speak French, and I made good grades in highschool. Nevertheless my best friend was chosen. She could not speak another language. Her aunt worked for the airline.*
Your activities (groups, clubs, org) in which you participate that confirms or supports belief	*Volunteered in groups that worked for equal rights in hiring during college*

How the Subconscious Mind Works

Now, let's look at the final result. Boxes 1, 3, and 4 may identify the precipitating person(s) or incident(s) that planted the belief seed. Not that the belief is right, wrong, good, or bad -- it is only to say that all beliefs have a beginning. We were not born with deeply-seated beliefs.

A belief often begins with the words or actions of an authority figure/role model or a life experience that is generalized as a truth for all similar experiences and situations.

Because the "knowledge" that a belief represents is precious and valuable, the belief is protected. That's the way the human psyche works. Boxes 2 and 5 represent preservation and perpetuation of the belief -- friends concur with (or at least tolerate) the belief and the believer. Then the believer seeks out activities, groups, clubs, and organizations that lend credence to his/her belief.

I believe that initially the mind's tendency to protect and preserve beliefs was a survival tool. Man learned how to start a fire, improved on the skills through trial and error, and later became an expert at fire starting; by remembering and internalizing the process. The process was now automated, given the proper tools.

A more modern example is riding a bicycle.

Bicycling is usually learned with the assistance of the child's primary role models and authority figures, mom and/or dad. The child learns how to ride with training wheels, and later without them. One day the child balances and rides alone into the sunset... Oh happy day!

Thirty-seven years later, after being off a bicycle for many years, the adult (now 45 years old) mounts a bicycle again. Miracle of miracles. He can ride without refresher lessons or parental assistance.

The bicycle miracle is the work of the subconscious mind, a deep level of the mind that is not open for daily inspection or sharing (without conscious effort). The subconscious mind is where we store learned activities and learned ideas (beliefs). Man in his magnificent capability for adaptation, soon adapted the ability to learn and automate physical processes. He applied that same ability to ideas and beliefs. Once man saw belief XYZ as an unquestionable truth, he stored it away as an infallible truth with which and through which all future decisions would be filtered. Nothing in the subconscious mind is "up for discussion". Everything deposited there is a "done deal" -- debated and decided. No call for change is welcome.

Just as the bicycle rider could fluently access the file on how to ride a bike 37 years later -- so the person deciding on a spouse can download his/her predetermined thoughts on love and marriage, and use that information to approve or reject a mate. The subconscious process can shorten the re-learning curve for physical activities to milliseconds. It can also decrease decision time for social decisions [like "Should this person be my friend?" or "Should this person be a candidate for marriage and lifelong partnership?" or "Will I ever marry? Is it safe?"]

As a repository for beliefs, the subconscious mind also acts as a filter through which our daily thoughts and decisions flow. Nothing is O.K.'d that does not fit with current beliefs. If subconscious beliefs are bypassed, the person sits in conflict and often unconsciously sabotages his own success.

It sounds complicated, and it is -- much more complicated than what I've told you. Just know that what you believe, deep inside, affects all that you do, and say, feel and decide -- even though you are no longer consciously aware of what's deep inside. It can be a trying task to bring what is deep inside to the surface where you can see it and examine it. That's why psychiatrists, psychologists and counselors get the big bucks.

For example: If I ask you your name, that information is right there on the tip of your tongue and your brain. So you give me an answer immediately. You are consciously aware of your name. But if I ask you, "What is your opinion on abortion?" You will hesitate and search your mind for an answer. You might not answer because you really don't know how you feel, but your real feelings about the matter are tucked away in your subconscious mind. You may lie just to get rid of the uncomfortable feeling -- or to keep from saying, "I don't know" [which really means I have not examined my deep thoughts and feelings on the subject. What I am immediately aware of in my mind does not suffice to answer such a weighty question].

Like the foundation of a building which goes deep into the ground and is mostly unseen -- the subconscious mind is not readily visible to you, but it supports and pretty much directs your life.

For clarity, let's review the example form like the one you have completed or will complete on page 19. Again, do not be offended. The example does not represent the author's beliefs, but is an extreme example for demonstration

Looking at this answer sheet we can see:

1. The person was exposed to people, as a child and as a teenager, who felt that hiring selections were based on having

a personal relationship with the person hiring.

2. The person had friends and relatives who agreed with or tolerated this view.
3. The person's belief was validated in the media by a movie that depicted the same ideas.
4. The person experienced a negative outcome in her own life that seemed unfair.
5. The person volunteered with groups that worked for equal rights in hiring practices.

The above experience is the stuff that beliefs are made of. Once activated and validated in the person's own mind, the belief is pretty much immovable and resists alteration. The belief seems plausible, but it is not universally valid. Just try changing her mind.

Insight, revelation, epiphany and even light -- these are not welcome in the realm of the subconscious mind. This realm prefers the deep-rooted, immutable, permanent, resolute, staying put, steadfast, solid as a rock, unfluctuating, and unwavering.

This is why it is so difficult for people to change their minds. Once a subconscious belief is challenged, a battle is required -- a battle between the current belief and new information or revelation. The subconscious mind views this as a battle for alteration to or removal of a belief that has been in place for some time, and perceives it as a potentially painful and even deadly process. Too often, today, that belief may be attached to an addiction. Addiction complicates change even further.

So where am I going with this psychological talk? I'm going to the heart of the matter. To change your path will likely require changing some of your beliefs and habits. In fact, it's inevitable.

The process of changing your mind may be painful -- and even deadly to your current beliefs. However, you've admitted that your current beliefs and modus operandi have not taken you where you desire to be. You may be so confused that you aren't even sure where you desire to be. Almighty God has already anticipated your fear and left you a message long ago:

> *Fear thou not; for I am with thee: be not dismayed; for I am thy God: I will strengthen thee; yea, I will help thee; yea, I will uphold thee with the right hand of my righteousness.*
> (Isa. 41:10 KJV)

A Basis for Future Examination

This chapter lays a foundation for exploration of your beliefs. You now have a format to use for examination of current beliefs. Current beliefs will always come forth from the recesses of the subconscious mind when a challenging belief system shows up. Like ancient knights, the opposing thought systems will joust to gain supremacy and veracity in the subconscious mind. Now you will be able to examine the origin of the dark knights, and to understand how you arrived at your iron-clad conclusions.

Not all of your beliefs are erroneous or bad. But if a belief has gotten you into trouble more than once, you need to trace it to its roots. The process of belief examination can be used whenever you want to find the origin of a belief you hold. Knowing the origin may help to determine the authenticity and value of the belief.

Be aware that new "iron-clad truths" can be accepted daily -- so guard your mind by diligent examination and strict entry criteria. Don't just let any old idea lodge in your head and your heart. Consider the source and think about it before accepting it.

> *Keep thy heart with all diligence;*
> *for out of it are the issues of life.*
> (Prov. 4:23 KJV)

Finally: **Not everything you believe deeply is true.** Some of it is downright wrong. Be open to change, especially if it means improvements in your life. Have faith that God has brought you to this point for a bonanza of blessing that starts with some mind changing on your part. Though you can't see, feel, or taste it -- have faith.

> *Now faith is the substance of things hoped for, the evidence of things not seen.* (Heb. 11:1 KJV)

Chapter Six

The Rocky Road of Life

Questions Answered

The questions were: "What should I think?" and "Can man even control the content of his thoughts? Isn't that just automatic?"

As to "What should I think?", the Bible tells us:

> *Finally, brethren, whatsoever things are true, whatsoever things are honest, whatsoever things are just, whatsoever things are pure, whatsoever things are lovely, whatsoever things are of good report; if there be any virtue, and if there be any praise, think on these things.* (Phil. 4:8 KJV)

In today's world the mind is bombarded with information via television, movies, books, music, and news reports. The majority of the input is not true, honest, just, pure, lovely, or of good report. The majority of what enters the mind does not contribute to virtue or praise.

As for the other two questions: "Can man even control the content of his thoughts? Isn't that just automatic?" Man can control the content of his thoughts by controlling what he allows into his mind. The old adage, "garbage in, garbage out" applies here. Negative, filthy, dishonest, pessimistic and impure input will manifest as negative, filthy, dishonest, pessimistic and impure thoughts -- and outcomes. Man must be ever-aware of what he allows to take root in his mind -- especially at the belief level. A thought might pass through, but one does not have to cultivate the thought into a belief. The thought can be dismissed and discarded.

Thoughts are not just automatic. Like the birds of a feather, they land where they feel comfortable -- with like thinkers and like thoughts. They tend to land and enter the heads wherein they are not challenged. If you are a negative thinker, negative thoughts will enter and fill your head. Positive thoughts will irk you. If you are paranoid, everyone you meet will appear to be against you. Put something new into that noggin, and you will have new thoughts.

Keep reading. This book contains new, positive thought material.

Mankind could use a washing of the mind, a purification and a starting all over **on purpose**. Men and women need to challenge accepted thought patterns and practices -- each beginning with him- or herself. The Bible speaks of *"... the washing of water by the word."* (Eph. 5:26 KJV) God's Word is a source of cleansing for the mind. God's Word is the only detergent that can remove spiritual and emotional smut and cleanse down to the level of the subconscious mind -- to challenge beliefs that the owner is not even aware of possessing.

The Bible urges us to change:

> *And be not conformed to this world: but be ye transformed by the renewing of your mind, that ye may prove what is that good, and acceptable, and perfect will of God.* (Rom.12:2 KJV)

There is only one way to renew (make new again) the mind. That is by hearing, reading, studying, and doing the Word of God.

Unfortunately, most people don't feel the need to inspect or challenge their beliefs, thoughts, or ways unless they collide head-on with insurmountable obstacles or life-altering problems. Then they may ask, "What am I do-ing wrong?" Often this question is being asked much too late. I am speaking to you, my reader, **now** -- before you hit a brick wall. I urge you to evaluate the rocky road upon which you've trodden until now.

Rocky Road Experience

The rocky road is not a delicious ice cream treat. The rocky road is the path or way that you walk upon today. It is your "do-it-yourself" formula for living life. It's the result of going through your life without acknowledging your Creator nor the words that He left for your in-struction and guidance. It's what you lovingly call *my way.*

- So how's the walk on you personalized rocky road?
- Is everything going well?
- Are those dreams coming true?
- Are you mistake-free?
- Is trial-and-error working well for you?
- How many times have you butted heads with fate?
- Have you had a near-death experience and survived?
- Have you been to jail or prison?

- Have you had an abortion?
- Have you overdosed on drugs or alcohol?
- Are you addicted and disappointing everyone who ever loved and had faith in you?
- Have you taken a human life (even though no one knows but you)?
- Are you misusing and being misused in turn?
- Are you confused?
- Are you lost? Are you in denial?

We tend to walk out our rocky road, even when we have no shoes on. We stoically persevere, hoping that *my way* will eventually work out, and all will know that I was right all along. Some walk the rocky road to the grave -- never sharing with the world the potential for good that God placed inside them. But well able to mutter in the end: *"I did it my way!"* That could be the epithet on the tombstone of every loser in the world.

My way is greatly over-rated! If it's not *The Way* it can lead to all of the mishaps listed above, and more... The rocky roads that we create for ourselves are born of ignorance. The Bible says: *My people are destroyed for lack of knowledge...* (Hosea 4:6 KJV)

The easiest thing to do is to fall in mindlessly

with the crowd (your chosen group) and do what everyone else is doing. No thought required. Just because the majority of people your age are doing it, doesn't make **IT** the right thing to do. As I progressed through life, I decided that usually the majority is wrong, or at least misled.

Believe me, I am not perfect and all wise. But I walk on *The Way*. I am renewing my mind. I do have unlimited access to all wisdom. So can you... And it's free!

I have struggled as you struggle. I have made countless mistakes and reaped the perilous outcomes of numerous misjudgments -- following my "do-it-yourself" formula for life.

That's why I'm sitting here with you -- talking to you. I want you to succeed. I want to help you find *The Way* to what you've been searching for. I don't judge you. I applaud you -- for making it this far, and for holding the answer in your hands.

Don't blow it brother. Don't miss this opportunity sister! Hold on tightly!

Chapter Seven

My Personal Journey

Young, Gifted, and Not so Smart

This is the hardest chapter to write. I am a very private person, and I rarely share my personal journey with others. It causes me pain and regret when those memories and emotions resurface. God has removed my sins and mistakes as far as the east is from the west. He remembers them no more. But people do not always understand that, and it gives them something to talk about and to feel superior about.

I will not go into all the gory details of my ignorance -- but I was a dummy. You would never have thought that I'd end up incarcerated for forgery and theft. But I was a dummy.

I joined a Christian church when I was around eight years old. My entire family attended that church, Eastside Baptist. My sister and I sang in the children's choir. I enjoyed learning about Jesus as a child, and I considered church as a great social experience. Sunday school, singing in the choir, and church picnics were great fun.

A few years later my family moved to an Apostolic/Pentecostal church where all members were expected to receive the gift of the Holy Ghost, with the evidence of "speaking in tongues". At the time, I didn't understand all the whys of that, but I did receive the gift, and I spoke another language.

I should stop calling myself a dummy. None of us were dummies. We were ignorant of the Truth. Each of us was lost in the darkness of this world. If you don't have light, you cannot see. There's no mystery about that, and there is no blame. We expect our parents to help us and teach us how to avoid pitfalls, but often they don't know *The Way* either. Just being a church member does not assure that you know *The Way*. Furthermore, new pitfalls are dug with each new generation. Even if our parents knew all, by age fifteen or sixteen we would not listen to them. The teenage period of rebellion causes many young people to disregard parental wisdom. Listening to one's parents might save a young person from unforeseeable misery and pain.

We each feel that we are different from

anyone else who was ever born. We want to do it *my way*. We stumble through our youth making mammoth mistakes that will color our lives forever. We drag the traps that caught us into our future. It is an opus magnum (great work) to disentangle ourselves from the snares and regret of the past.

You know, it is amazing that I was such a smart kid, but such an ignorant adult. Book smarts don't magically translate into "street smarts". I was put into a program for gifted children at the age of eleven. I was the only black student in my class. The racism was thick in the atmosphere, but I breathed that air of distaste and excelled anyhow. I stayed in the program from grade six through grade eight. Boy did that mess with my self-esteem. (This took place in the sixties, when everyone thought African Americans were still slaves and couldn't possibly have a brain.) The kids in my neighborhood teased me and called me names because I did not go to the local school. I often felt alone despite my three siblings. Then I went to high school, which was uneventful for the most part.

Backslidden

I credit church membership for taking me pretty safely through my teens. By the age of seventeen, I became disillusioned with the church. I learned that some of the church members were not living a Christian life. Their acts were scandalous. With that information, added to my raging hormones, I did the unthinkable. I became a "backslider", and I left the church.

After high school, I started college, but the end of the first semester coincided with my "backslide", so I went *AWOL* into oblivion.

I hit the streets wild and furious -- feeling like I had missed out on many good years of my life in that "stupid church" where everyone was a hypocrite, and the rules did not make sense. The streets were waiting for yet another innocent like me -- gullible and unfamiliar with the territory and its mores.

I was still a virgin at the time, saving myself for my marriage partner. That did not last too long. Inevitably I chose the wrong mates -- one after another. Each taught me a new bad habit. Each led me further away from God. Each instilled his erroneous beliefs, and I was a willing recipient of the garbage thoughts. I married one of them. It lasted eight months before the divorce. My reward was a beautiful baby girl.

At any rate, I progressed to sexual immorality, drugs, and finally jail. That's where I awoke and began reparation and reconciliation. But it wasn't over.

Reparation and Reconciliation

I restarted my education. Shortly after release from jail, I received a bachelor's degree. (I worked on the degree while incarcerated.) With the help of Almighty God, I later received two master's degrees. I'm not bragging -- just emphasizing that God's touch can change your heart, your mind and your life. Since that time, I have never wanted for a job nor for adequate compensation.

In 1979, I married a man from my past who was a drug addict and mentally unstable. (I didn't realize that he was still on drugs. I did not know he was mentally unstable. After all, I was off drugs and not mentally unstable -- just naive.) I believed that he had also progressed. The horror stories are too many to recount in this book. Suffice it to say that this was not a match made in heaven. That mistake netted me a genius son and another beautiful daughter. All of my children are very smart, but my son could read a newspaper at age eighteen months, without assistance. (Refer to my first book, *Teaching Our Babies to Read*, for details.)

I returned to the church in 2000. At Living Word Christian Center, I was able to learn a lot about the Bible, about God, and about myself. All of the answers we need are in the book -- the Holy Bible. I attribute much of my spiritual growth and development to the teachings of Pastor Bill Winston.

Once I accepted Jesus Christ, my marriage became worse. My mate hated my newfound Christian faith and taunted me unceasingly. He was sadistic anyhow, but my faith allowed opportunity for a new level of psychological warfare. I divorced my husband after 25 years of mistreatment. By then my three children were adults.

I study God's Word and pray every day. That doesn't mean I'm perfect or pious. It means I am on *The Way*. I believe that God has ordained me to write, to help others find *The Way*. The world is a murky and dark place to navigate without guidance. Sometimes one word, especially a word from God, can change the life and light up the existence of a man or woman. It's all so much better when you can see.

I have never regretted my entry into *The Way*. I have peace, joy, and power in my relationship with God. He offers each of us unconditional love and forgiveness. He promises us grace (un-merited favor) and victory. I am no longer a loser. I am victorious in Christ Jesus!

The information in this chapter provides a skeletal view of my life. Perhaps at some point in the future I will be brave enough to fill in the gaps with the full story. I pray God that the little

I have revealed will give me credibility as one who was also lost. Nothing in this book is meant to make the reader feel ashamed about life up until this point. We all struggle until we have light to guide us. The light is the Word of God

> *Thy word is a lamp unto my feet, and*
> *a light unto my path.* (Ps.119:105 KJV)

Verse 130 of Psalm119 says:

> *The entrance of thy words giveth light;*
> *it giveth understanding unto the sim-*
> *ple.* (Ps.119:130 KJV)

After hearing about my struggle, you may feel like a saint. My life was not a pretty picture. My choices were those of another rat lost in the maze of life. *The Way* was always available. I had come into contact with it as a child -- but I rejected it as below my intellect, "an opiate for the people" as Karl Marx called it. I was determined that I would not be part of the down-trodden masses that cowered in the shadows of religion for solace.

Not a good choice on my part!

Ironically, I was the most down-trodden of all. I was a poor, pitiable lost soul looking for **real** answers in the most **unreal** places. They included sexual promiscuity, alcohol, drugs, and criminal activities. (And to be honest, I have not revealed all of my past vices here.) I ran from situation to situation, assured that I was a player who understood the way of the streets. Everyone who disagreed with my philosophy was a square (or what young people today call a nerd). I was miserable, but I would never admit it. Neither would I confess that I was lost.

I thank God for rescuing my life from destruction.

> *Bless the Lord, O my soul: and all that is within me, bless his holy name. Bless the Lord, O my soul, and forget not all his benefits: who forgiveth all thine iniquities; who healeth all thy diseases; who redeemeth thy life from destruction; who crowneth thee with lovingkindness and tender mercies;...*
> (Ps.103:1-4 KJV)

Chapter Eight

Decision Point

Here I give the reader a chance to opt out. If you have read all that precedes this chapter, and you think that the content of this book does not apply to you -- then you may decide not to read the remainder of this book. I suggest that you finish this chapter by answering the questions below. Then decide.

1. Do you have peace in your life that passes all understanding?
2. Do you have love in your heart for others?
3. Do you have love in your heart for all mankind?
4. Have you forgiven all of the people who have hurt you, harmed you, disagreed with you, deceived you, or lied to you?
5. Do you know God?

6. Do you clearly know what's right and wrong?

7. Are you wise?

8. Do you feel like you know all you need to know?

9. Do you know why your were born?

10. Do you feel condemned because of past or present actions?

11. Do you feel guilty because of past or present actions?

12. Does your conscience bother you because of past or present actions?

13. Do you feel like you have to get even with those who wronged you?

14. Do you feel lost?

15. Do you feel confused?

16. Do you think about hurting yourself?

17. Do you think about hurting someone else?

18. Do you feel unloved?

19. Are you hurting right now?

20. Are your thoughts in turmoil most of the time?

21. Do you want to drop this book and run?

22. Are you picking up this book again after several weeks or months?

If you answered "NO" to even one of the questions numbered 1 through 9, then you definitely **should not** opt out. If you answered "YES" to even one of questions 10 through 22, then you must continue reading this book.

The Spirit of God decided the questions I should ask above. If even one of these questions hits home for you, then this book was sent to help rescue you. I am not the rescuer. This book is not even the rescuer. God is the One who rescues lives from pain, confusion, turmoil, guilt, hatred, and unforgiveness. **He loves you individually.** He knows your name. This book has some answers that you need. This book is guidance to *The Way*. Follow these crumbs of knowledge to your destiny. God has a plan for your life. I'm praying for you.

> *For I know the thoughts that I think toward you, saith the Lord, thoughts of peace, and not of evil, to give you an expected end.* (Jer. 29:11 KJV)

Chapter Nine

Choose Life

Way Out, Way In

The way out is through the way in. That's a paradox -- a phrase that seems to contradict itself. Hansel and Gretel [the fairytale characters] got it. They dropped bread crumbs as they walked, so that they could find their way back home [just in case this trip into the dark forest was not a good idea]. A good plan!

However, it was a good plan that did not account for all the unforeseen variables. Hansel and Gretel did not count on birds eating their bread crumb trail. When they wanted to go back the way they came [after meeting the witch with the gingerbread house], there were no markers to show them the way.

Retracing your steps backwards sounds like a plausible solution, but only if you are absolutely sure of the way you came. Many of us, probably most of us, end up at the witch's house -- that looked so delightful from afar, but close-up is ominous and down-right scary. Most of you can't even imagine how you got to where you are. You might recall one or two major events, but you can't remember all of the little twists and turns you took along the way. Retracing your steps is not possible. You need divine intervention -- or into the witch's crockpot you go! Dinner for the dark side!

The Solution

Enough about the problem(s). Let's start talking solution. How does one get out of a mess like yours? What's the way out?

Well, since the bread crumbs are gone, and you can't remember every detail of how you got into this mess; I would suggest a radical shift as the solution. If you continue to aimlessly meander on your current path, it can only get worse. So why not just change paths altogether. Fool the enemy with an unexpected change of direction. Today God has created for you a fork in the road -- a crossroad. Make a choice for life.

See I have set before thee this day life and good, and death and evil;...

> *I call heaven and earth to record this day against you, that I have set before you life and death, blessing and cursing: therefore choose life, that both thou and thy seed may live:...*
> (Deut. 30:15, 19 KJV)

God is offering a choice today, right now. Do you prefer life and good or death and evil? God is commanding heaven and earth to record your decision. This decision is that big a deal. Do you want life or death? Blessing or cursing? God recommends that you choose life so that you and your seed (your children) can live.

Do you have children? That adds an entirely different dimension and gravity to your decisions -- this decision and all others. You have another life or other lives that will be affected by what you do and every choice you make in life. Have you ever considered the children -- your offspring or the other young people who love you (nieces, nephews, young impressionable cousins, young impressionable siblings)?

For now, all you have to do is say: **"I choose life!"** No more. No less. That short sentence lets all parties know that you are serious and that you are about to make a radical shift in your life. God hears you. The angels hear you. Anyone nearby hears you.

"Is that all I have to do?" you ask. As I said above, that's all you have to do *for now.* That simple sentence is powerful, and it changes some things by its power. Heaven is poised for the fullness of your decision to be spoken. In the meantime you have informed heaven and earth that you choose life over death, good over evil, blessing over cursing. The powers that have worked against you have to pause and consider what you might do next. A return to the old way confirms their continued power over your life. A full move to *The Way* cancels their power over you and your life. The universe is watching. Nothing to fear, friend. Just want you to know that by choosing life you have initiated a powerful spiritual apparatus in your life. Praise God!

Say it again, loudly: **"I choose life!"**

Chapter Ten

The Crossroad

Next Step

In the modern business world, a much-used term to plan and solve problems involves the phrase "next steps". At the end of the meeting or problem-solving session, the group leader reviews the meeting and asks: "What are the next steps?" The replies to that question guide the group's activities until they meet again. The "next steps" also become the goals to measure progress at the next meeting.

In the next chapter, I will first give you some background information. This information will assist you to speak your decision with under-standing later. You've set the tone and laid some powerful groundwork by choosing life, but you're not finished. It's as if you said in high school, "I'm going to run track this year", but you haven't said what you're going to run -- sprints, ¼ mile, ½ mile, long 5 mile runs or what. And before you make such a decision you need some more information.

So our next steps are: (1) presentation of background information and (2) consideration of the full decision to be spoken later.

A word first... This process is faith-based. You must have faith in the invisible God and His love for you. Oh! -- you think that's a stretch? You had faith in your parents who threw you out. You had faith in your "friends" who lied to you, stole from you, and tricked you into illegal activities that landed you in jail. You had faith in your girlfriend or boyfriend who left you for the first pretty face that smiled at them. You had faith in sexual promiscuity that left you with STDs (sexually transmitted diseases) and maybe even HIV. You had faith in alcohol to take away your pain, but you only got blackouts and DUI's in exchange. You had faith in marijuana, heroine, crack-cocaine, meth -- until you woke up in the gutter, without friends or family or any means of support.

Rest for Your Soul

This moment is the crossroad. Some may back away now, even though God is calling. It's happened before in the lives of men and women from ancient times to this moment. God brings a man or woman to *The Way*, and they say to God: I am not going to walk that way. I'm going to follow my own way. His Word speaks of a very similar incident in Jeremiah 6. I'm going to share three translations of this scripture: King James Version, NIV, and the Message Bible. The three forms will, hopefully, make clear what God is saying to you.

> *Thus saith the Lord, Stand ye in the ways and see, and ask for the old paths, where is the good way, and walk therein, and ye shall find rest for your souls,but they said, We will not walk therein.* (Jer. 6 :16 KJV)

God's message yet again:

> *Go stand at the crossroads and look around.*
> *Ask for directions to the old road,*
> *The tried and true road. Then take it.*
> *Discover the right route for your souls.*
> *But they said, 'Nothing doing.*
> *We aren't going that way.'*
> (Jer. 6:16 *NIV/The Message Parallel Study Bible.* Grand Rapids, MI: Zondervan, 2008)

This is what the Lord says:
Stand at the crossroads and look;
ask for the ancient paths
ask where the good way is, and walk in it,
and you will find rest for your souls.
But you said, "We will not walk in it."
(Jer. 6:16 *NIV/The Message* 2008)

In this scripture, God is offering "rest for your souls" and the "right route for your souls", yet the offer is being refused. Doesn't that rest sound good? Aren't you tired of struggling and suffering? Aren't you tired of stumbling and falling? Aren't you tired of failure and defeat? Aren't you weary of the enemy's abuse?

We've come too far together for you to give up now. You've tried everything else on your journey. Give God a chance.

I know you have questions. I know you've seen and heard of bad examples of "Christians". "Hypocrites" you call them. Your questions will be answered, and that poor behavior and hypocrisy will be explained -- maybe not all in this book, but in future ones. Don't let the behaviors of misguided and insincere folk prevent your soul solution. As in any human endeavor, there are those who do it right and those who do it wrong. Just compare a Yugo and a Lexus. Both are cars, but the finished product is totally different in appearance and functioning.

"Churches just want money." I'm not a church, and I don't want your money. You don't ever have to give a dime to a church, unless you want to. Salvation is free. Jesus already paid the price. Don't be distracted or delayed by stereotypical assumptions you've heard all your life.

Chapter Eleven

Foundation for Salvation

The Beginning

It is always best to make important decisions with background and foundational knowledge in hand. Let's start at the very beginning:

> *In the beginning God created the heaven and the earth.* (Gen. 1:1 KJV)

God created the world with words. He spoke "Let there be..." and whatever He named came into existence. Adam, the first man, was created in God's image and likeness -- meaning that Adam operated just like God.

> *And God said, Let us make man in our own image, after our likeness: and let them have dominion over the fish of the*

sea, and over the fowl of the air, and
over the cattle, and over all the earth,
and every creeping thing that creepeth
upon the earth.

So God created man in his own Image,
in the image of God created He him;
male and female created he them.
(Gen.1:26-27 KJV)

Adam was given dominion over the whole earth.
It was his birthright given to him by Almighty
God. No one could argue with Adam's right
to dominion. Nothing could challenge Adam's
right to rule, except disobedience to God.

God gave Adam a female companion. Adam
named her Eve.

And the Lord God caused a deep sleep
to fall upon Adam, and he slept: and he
took one of his ribs, and closed up the
flesh thereof;

And the rib, which the Lord God had
taken from man, made he a woman,
and brought her unto the man.
(Gen. 2:21-22 KJV)

God had already given Adam some command-ments to abide by:

> *And the Lord God commanded the man, saying, of every tree of the garden thou mayest freely eat:*

> *But of the tree of the knowledge of good and evil, thou shalt not eat of it: for in the day that thou eatest thereof thou shalt surely die.* (Gen. 2:16-17 KJV)

The Deception and The Fall

All was well in the garden of Eden. There was no sickness and no death. Eating of the tree of knowledge of good and evil would activate the penalty for disobedience -- bringing death into man's world. That act of disobedience and the corresponding consequences brought the knowledge of good and evil. Prior to this act, there was only good for man.

> *Now the serpent was more subtil than any beast of the field which the Lord God had made. And he said unto the woman, Yea, hath God said, Ye shall not eat of every tree of the garden?*

*And the woman said unto the serpent,
We may eat of the fruit of the trees of
the garden:*

*But of the fruit of the tree which is in
the midst of the garden, God hath said,
Ye shall not eat of it, neither shall ye
touch it, lest ye die.*

*And the serpent said unto the woman,
Ye shall not surely die: For God doth
know that in the day ye eat thereof,
then your eyes shall be opened, and
ye shall be as gods, knowing good and
evil.*

*And when the woman saw that the
tree was good for food, and that it was
pleasant to the eyes, and a tree to be
desired to make one wise, she took of
the fruit thereof, and did eat, and gave
also unto her husband with her; and he
did eat.* (Gen. 3:1-6 KJV)

The enemy, satan, tricked Eve, and Adam followed her lead. The consequences of Adam and Eve's decision was grave -- not only for them, but for all mankind, including you and I. All descendants, even up to the present generation are born into sin and live under the curses spoken on the lives of Adam and Eve. Adam and Eve were evicted from the beautiful, pristeen garden of Eden. God spoke this curse:

> *Unto the woman he said, I will greatly multiply thy sorrow and thy conception; in sorrow thou shalt bring forth children, and thy desire shall be to thy husband, and he shall rule over thee.*
>
> *And unto Adam he said, Because thou hast hearkened unto the voice of thy wife, and hast eaten of the tree, of which I commanded thee, saying, Thou shalt not eat of it: cursed is the ground for thy sake; in sorrow shalt thou eat of it all the days of thy life;*
>
> *Thorns also and thistles shall it bring forth to thee; and thou shalt eat the herb of the field;*
>
> *In the sweat of thy face shalt thou eat bread, till thou return unto the ground; for out of it wast thou taken: for dust thou art, and unto dust shalt thou return.* (Gen. 3:16-19 KJV)

And these were but physical manifestations of the curse. There were spiritual ramifications as well. The law of sin and death ruled mankind after Adam's disobedience, -- and continued to rule mankind until God provided a solution. The solution is Jesus Christ. Just as all mankind became sinners with the act of Adam, so each man can become righteous by the act of Jesus Christ.

> *For as by one man's disobedience many were made sinners, so by the obedience of one shall many be made righteous.* (Rom. 5:19 KJV)

Adam had dominion over the earth, but he handed that birthright over to satan. By doing so, he lost peace, joy, and his life of rest.

Redemption

With acceptance and belief in Jesus Christ as your savior, you can walk in the law of the Spirit of life in Jesus Christ. You can trade death for life. You can reclaim peace and joy. You can be free.

> *For the law of the Spirit of life in Christ Jesus hath made me free from the law of sin and death.* (Rom. 8:2 KJV)

Jesus Christ came to earth and lived a life without sin. Instead of being embraced by those who called themselves men of God, he was rejected, persecuted, and finally killed. After three days, by God's resurrection power, Jesus arose from the dead. Jesus taught his disciples for 40 days and then ascended into heaven. He sits at the right hand of God and intercedes (prays) for you and I. By the blood of Jesus Christ you are redeemed from the law of sin and death. You only need to choose life by declaring your allegiance to Jesus and accepting the free gift of salvation. Jesus is saying to you now:

> ...*I am **the way**, the truth, and the life: no man cometh unto the Father, but by me.* (John 14:6 KJV)

Each of us has a choice -- to remain in sin and death or to enter *The Way* by accepting Jesus Christ. This book is not meant to be a full discourse on the sins of Adam and the blessed life of Jesus -- the son of God. This book is an introduction to *The Way*. To begin is important....

Jesus redeemed us from the curse caused by Adam's disobedience. Jesus takes away all of our sin. Like a watch purchased from a pawn shop, we are redeemed by the sacrifice of Jesus Christ.

If you are hearing this news for the first time,

it may seem too easy and too miraculous to be true. **But it is true!** Right now, this hour, you can lay down every burden of sin and guilt that you have been dragging around for years. You can give it all to Jesus and change your life forever.

> *Therefore if any man be in Christ, he is a new creature: old things are passed away; behold all things are become new.* (2 Cor. 5:17 KJV)

Today's world wants to make everything complicated and difficult to achieve. But God has made it simple to enter into *The Way*. You don't need multiple degrees or internships. You don't have to go on a cleansing diet or memorize a book. You don't have to injure yourself to prove you're serious. You don't have to travel around the world to find a guru. All you have to do is speak and believe what you're saying. God will do the rest.

Jesus changes your life for the good. He changes your desires. He changes your behavior. He changes your actions and activities. He gives you peace, and joy. He gives you power. He gives you wisdom and understanding. He teaches you how to forgive and how to love. He teaches you how to control your emotions. He takes away the desire for unseemly conduct and perversion.

As you begin to read the Bible, it may seem foggy and incomprehensible. But as you continue to read and study, your perseverance will be rewarded with clear understanding. I remember picking up a Bible in times past. I opened it, and it sounded like Chinese or Swahili to me. It made no sense. Now I can flow through it with understanding. Every time I read the Bible I see wisdom that I missed before. It's almost like it multiplies in meaning the more you read it.

I've heard ministers say that God created us and that the Bible is the owner's manual for man. It is **the** roadmap and guidebook to help you find and walk in *The Way*.

Dear reader, begin now! Allow these words to point you out of the wilderness *where there is no way* (Ps.107:40 KJV). Let God *teach you his way* (Ps. 86:11 KJV). You have already said, **"I choose life!"** Now I urge you to say aloud the prayer at the end of this chapter -- which seals your commitment to enter *The Way*. Do you have commitment issues? This prayer will be the most valued commitment of your life. Let me assure you this prayer brings you into covenant (contract) with Almighty God Himself. What a privilege! What an opportunity! You will never walk alone again.

Be strong and of a good courage; be not afraid, neither be thou dismayed: for the Lord thy God is with thee whither-soever thou goest. (Josh. 1:9 KJV)

The same scripture from the Message translation reads:

Strength! Courage! Don't be timid: don't get discouraged. God, your God, is with you every step you take. (Josh. 1:9 The Message)

By choosing life, you took the first step. To complete your decision and fully speak your commitment to God, say the following prayer *aloud*. Read it sincerely, believing that your life is about to change -- because it is.

Dear Lord, I come to you now, just as I am.
You know my life. You know how I've lived.
Forgive me Lord. I repent of my sins.
I believe that Jesus Christ is the Son of God.
He died for my sins. On the third day,
he was raised from the dead.
Lord Jesus, I ask you to come into my heart.
Live your life in me and through
me from now on.
From this day forward, I belong to you.
In the Name of Jesus. Amen.

WELCOME TO THE WAY!

Chapter Twelve

Welcome to The Way

Be Thankful

Congratulations! If you said that prayer, you have moved from the path of sin and death to *The Way*. *The Way* is the path of the Spirit of life in Christ Jesus. You have moved from death to life; from defeat to victory; from depression to joy; from evil to good; from old to new. If you're crying now, it's o.k. It took a tremendous amount of courage and faith to accept Jesus on His word. But the rewards make it worthwhile. Bask in the joy and peace that you are experiencing now. Say "**Thank You Jesus**" to voice your gratitude to the Lord for bringing you this far.

So, there was no one with you to witness your prayer? Makes no difference! All of heaven is your witness. All of heaven is rejoicing for your salvation. I am rejoicing for your salvation!

Yes, begin with thanks. Always be grateful to God for everything that He does for you every day. Even the things you may take for granted, like food, water, and a roof over your head. Be thankful and say so. I've travelled to many countries where food and clean water are not a given. I've seen people sleeping under tarps and in the open air without cover. I've seen small children begging for crumbs to eat. I've seen people without adequate covering against the elements. Let God know you are grateful, and that you know that He is responsible for your good fortune. The fool takes these things for granted, but the wise man knows from whence his blessings come. Let this be the first manifestation of your new wisdom.

In your city, town, village or circumstance, try to find a place to worship God -- a chapel or a church, or perhaps Bible classes. Ask God for guidance, so that you choose the best place for your development. If the church or facility you choose has the capability, you should be baptized in the name of Jesus. Try to find a location that can accommodate baptism and receiving of the Holy Ghost (also called Holy Spirit).

> *Then Peter said unto them, Repent, and be baptized every one of you in the name of Jesus Christ for the*

> *remission [forgiveness] of sins, and ye*
> *shall receive the gift of the Holy Ghost.*
> (Acts 2:38 KJV) [Author's emphasis]

From this moment forward, your real food is spiritual. I am not encouraging anyone not to eat natural food. That would be crazy. What I'm saying is that you now have to feed your spirit, as well as your body. Your inner being is nourished by the Word of God. If you don't have access to a place of worship, try to obtain books, audiotapes, CDs or DVDs of sermons and Bible teachings. There are also regular television broadcasts of Bible instruction on the Trinity Broadcasting Network (TBN), Daystar, and The Word stations. There are probably other local stations in your area. You need spiritual food as crucially as you need bread, meat, fruits, and vegetables. The Word is a spiritual requirement for healthy spiritual growth and the renewal of your mind.

Renewal of my mind? Yes, renewal. Romans 12 tells us about this requirement:

> *And be not conformed to this world:*
> *but be ye transformed by the renewing*
> *of your mind, that ye may prove what*
> *is that good, and acceptable, and per-*
> *fect, will of God.* (Rom. 2:12 KJV)

The Holy Spirit (Holy Ghost)

Dear reader, your spirit was changed instantaneously by your acceptance of Jesus Christ as your Lord and Savior. However, there is work to be done with your mind and body. Up to this point, your mind, body and your emotions have done the decision-making in your life. As we established early on, this has not worked out well. You have previously been driven by ideas that are not even your own, but came from authority figures, media, friends, and bad experiences. Now it's time to let your spirit man (your inner man) take a leading role. Your mind and emotions must be submitted to the spirit. You'll be happy to know that your spirit is not working alone. When you accept Jesus, the Holy Spirit of God becomes an ally and moves in -- right inside of you. Remember that the Holy Ghost and the Holy Spirit are the same entity, depending on the translator.

> *But the Comforter, which is the Holy Ghost, whom the Father will send in my name, he shall teach you all things, and bring all things to your remembrance, whatsoever I have said unto you.* (John 14:26 KJV)

> *What? Know ye not that your body is*
> *the temple of the Holy Ghost which is*
> *in you, which ye have of God, and ye*
> *are not your own?* (1 Cor. 6:19 KJV)

The Holy Ghost (Holy Spirit) helps you, leads you, and teaches you. The Holy Ghost is God's Spirit living inside of you. This is not something weird, but rather an opportunity for sweet, daily, ongoing communion with God. Confirmation of receipt of the Holy Ghost is "speaking in tongues". If you don't have this confirmation experience right now, just know that the Spirit is there.

> *And they were all filled with the Holy*
> *Ghost, and began to speak with other*
> *tongues, as the Spirit gave them utter-*
> *ance.* (Acts 2:4 KJV)

> *And these signs shall follow them that*
> *believe; In my name shall they cast*
> *out devils; they shall speak with new*
> *tongues…* (Mark 16:17 KJV)

Not all churches and denominations teach the evidence of "speaking in tongues", but as you can see, it is Biblical. For me, it has been a source of power and comfort throughout my Christian life. I recommend this experience to all new and old Christians. God has provided this source of power for us, but we have to take advantage of it. The Holy Ghost is part of Jesus' promises to the disciples -- and to us. Pray to God for this promised gift, and He will provide it.

The Intellect

Listen friend, the following quotation is a word directly from God to me -- placed here to destroy a stronghold of doubt. By the way, a stronghold is a set of erroneous ideas that creates distorted thought patterns which a person believes are truth. If you are an intellectual (even an undercover intellectual), these words especially apply to you. No judgment. I've always been tempted to doubt by intellectualism, but I couldn't reason my way out of a crackerjack box without Jesus. God spoke these words to me:

"The intellectual has the need to run My Word through the constructs of analysis taught by the world. But those constructs cannot comprehend things which are spiritual in essence. These worldly ways of seeing can only distort the Word in order to form it into preset carnal/scientific frameworks that make them palatable to modern intellect -- to conform them to the word of man's limited wisdom. Once squeezed into erroneous

format, the words loose power and significance for the soul." (My Prayer Journal, 10/19/12)

Speaking of the Holy Spirit, in 1 Corinthians we read:

> *But the natural man receiveth not the things of the Spirit of God: for they are foolishness unto him: neither can he know them, because they are spiritually discerned.* (1 Cor.2:14 KJV)

This scripture is telling us that it is difficult for the physical man, the part of man which is not spiritual, to understand. Why should I even want a Holy Ghost or Holy Spirit to live in me? How is that even possible? That sounds like foolishness and hocus pocus! It's difficult to receive upon first glance. But you have accepted Jesus Christ, and you now have the power to spiritually discern (or understand) outside of your intellect and worldly input. There is more than appears to the natural eye in this world. Trust God and just follow His instructions. *The Way* stands before you. Have faith in God.

For those who did not pray that prayer of salvation at the end of Chapter 11, let me bring you an added message.

The highway of the upright is to depart from evil: he that keepeth his way preserveth his soul. (Prov. 16:17 KJV)

When a man departs from evil, (*i.e.* chooses the path of righteousness instead of the path of destruction); he is on the high way. He is on the highway of the upright. He is preserving his soul.

All of us are seeking and have been seeking. As noted in the Introduction of this book, the name we give to the object of our quest varies by culture, education, religious affiliation, and experience. But we all are searching and striving to obtain the unknown factor. Jeremiah speaks of the search:

> *And ye shall seek me, and find me, when ye shall search for me with all your heart.*
>
> *And I will be found of you, saith the Lord: and I will turn away your captivity...* (Jer. 29:13-14a KJV)

Even with no knowledge of this Bible scripture, and often without the knowledge that we are "searching", we pursue and search and experiment -- we get ourselves into a lot of problems and entanglements by looking under every rock and exploring every cave of life. Perhaps this book will prove to be a shortcut for you, if you are open to that voice that is speaking to you now and coaxing you to dig deeper.

Sometimes people do not know what they are looking for. They have assigned no name to the elusive object of fulfillment. They do not know in which life domain to focus attention --

- Home and family?
- Religion?
- Education?
- Self-analysis (am I doing something wrong)?
- Relationships?
- Occultism?
- Drugs?
- Alcohol?
- Sexual immorality?

1 Thessalonians adds some clarification:

> *For God hath not called us unto uncleanness, but unto holiness.*
> (1 Thess. 4:7 KJV)

There's little that is more fulfilling than being in the perfect will of God. Several of the domains above can be crossed off the search list. Occultism, drugs, alcoholism, and sexual immorality are not domains of God. They do not contribute to holiness.

Don't squander this opportunity.

> *Seek ye the Lord while he may be found, call ye upon him while he is near: Let the wicked forsake his way, and the unrighteous man his thoughts: and let him return unto the Lord, and he will have mercy upon him, and to our God, for he will abundantly pardon.*
> (Isa. 55: 6-7 KJV)

The reading of this book is a call to life. God speaks further in Isaiah 55

> *Incline your ear, and come unto me: hear, and your soul shall live;...*
> (Isa.55:3a KJV)

God loves you. He is calling to you personally. God wants to give you peace and joy. But you must recognize and listen to His voice. If you haven't already, go to the last page of chapter 11 and read out loud the prayer of salvation, in Jesus' Name. Other opportunities to accept Jesus are not promised.

Chapter Thirteen

A Call for Restoration

A Call for Restoration

Why did I ask you to speak the confession in acceptance of Jesus Christ as your Lord and Savior? You had to, because Jesus is *The Way*.

> *Jesus saith unto him, I am the way, the truth, and the life: no man cometh unto the Father, but by me.* (John 14:6 KJV)

And notice in John 14 Jesus says: ...*but the Father that dwelleth in me, he doeth the works.* (John 14:10 KJV) Jesus' work included the words he spoke and the miracles he performed. He said that God was dwelling in Him.

Now God dwells in you, in the form of the Holy Spirit. He will also speak to you and through you. He will teach you directly. He will use you to do miraculous works. Jesus was a carpenter by trade, and yet He became the most influential man who ever walked this earth. His influence continues powerfully today.

My friend, just take a leap of faith. God has plans for your life. Try believing what the Word of God says, and follow the footsteps of Jesus.

> *For I know the thoughts that I think toward you, saith the Lord, thoughts of peace, and not of evil, to give you an expected end.*
>
> *And ye shall seek me, and find me, when ye shall search for me with all your heart.* (Jer. 29: 11, 13 KJV)

Search to know God, with all your heart. He promises that you will find Him if you do so. God already has an "expected end" or destiny for you -- and He says that this end is not an evil one. No matter what you have done in your life, God forgave you when you spoke that prayer of faith.

Do you feel like you've been a prisoner of circumstances or trapped in a hole (or pattern of behavior) with no way to climb out? Listen to what God says:

But this is a people robbed and spoiled;
they are all of them snared in holes,
and they are hid in prison houses: they
are for a prey, and none delivereth;
for a spoil, and none saith, Restore.
(Isa. 42:22 KJV)

Right now, I say RESTORE! I decree that your life is changed. I decree that old habits die, taking with them the very desire. I decree that your mind is washed by the Word of God and renewed. I decree that you are transformed from this day forward. I decree that you are free. I decree that you find rest and full deliverance from whatever chains have bound you in your life. I decree that you climb out of that hole of despair. I decree that every prison door opens. I decree that relationships are restored and healed. I decree that you are a new creature in Jesus Christ. I decree that you fulfill your expected end. In the Name of Jesus Christ of Nazareth. Amen.

Chapter Fourteen

Heavenly Assistants

Angels

The Way leads to your destination -- your destiny. Some of you have an inkling of what your destiny is. Others have no clue. But know that you are on this earth to do something worthwhile. Biographies and autobiographies are excellent for inspiration and encouragement. They show that you can overcome and succeed despite problems, weaknesses, and obstacles. However, they are not maps to be followed without question. Each design is different. God created each of us as a unique being with an individualized purpose. No one else can fill your intended role, and you should not try to copy or fill another's designated spot. God has already prepared your place. You just need to get there. Exodus 23:20 reads:

> *Behold, I send an angel before thee, to*
> *keep thee in the way, and to bring thee*
> *into the place which I have prepared.*
> (Exod. 23:20 KJV)

The Comforter

God has even provided assistance in the form of an angel. Then God gives you a helper and guide, the Holy Spirit. As mentioned a few pages back, Jesus prophesied the coming of the Holy Spirit. In the Amplified version of the Bible, this scripture describes the Holy Spirit:

> *But the Comforter (Counselor, Helper,*
> *Intercessor, Advocate, Strengthener,*
> *Standby), the Holy Spirit, Whom the*
> *Father will Send in My name [in My*
> *place, to represent Me and act on My*
> *behalf], He will teach you all things.*
> *And He will cause you to recall (will*
> *remind you of, bring to your remem-*
> *brance) everything I have told you.*
> (John 14:26 AMP)

It is clear here that Jesus means for the Holy Spirit to comfort, strengthen, help, pray for, and stand by you. The Holy Spirit is a counselor and helps you remember the Word of God that you hear, read, and meditate.

Daily Bread

The Word of God is your bread. It feeds your inner man. Your spirit has probably starved for years, even decades. The Word of God strengthens the part of your being that should rightfully be in control of your life. Rather than your mind or your body, or your emotions being in control of your life -- your inner man, your spirit, should be in charge. Your spirit has the ability to communicate directly with God through the Holy Spirit. All of your answers and decisions need to come from God through your spirit. That can alleviate trial and error.

Violent acts against others or against the property of others reflect an uncontrolled body. We have already talked about the unreliability of human thoughts, ideas, ideals, and beliefs -- when based on erroneous input from many possible sources. Unfettered emotions can move the body and the mind to unspeakable acts in a fit of passion.

God confirms man's three-part being in 1 Thessalonians.

And the very God of peace sanctify you wholly; and I pray God your whole spirit and soul and body be preserved blameless unto the coming of Our Lord Jesus Christ. (1 Thess. 5:23 KJV)

Throughout the Bible, heart is used to indicate your spirit. Your soul contains your mind, will, and your emotions. Your mind is your thinking mechanism. I look at the mind as the playground of the devil. It's the battleground where light and darkness battle daily. Other authors and ministers cover the content and functions of the soul and mind in detail. I cannot offer that detail at this time. Just know that your goal is to give all of the power to your spirit, and not to be ruled by your body, will, emotions, or your mind. Your mind is helpful. Without it you could not read this book. However, your spirit -- was created to be in charge of the body and the soul.

God Does the Work

By this time you might be saying, "This sounds hard. I've never even thought about controlling my mind or my body; let alone my emotions. Too hard. I might as well stop this really hard stuff right now."

What you, and most Christians (who may

have been Christians for years) don't know is that you don't do the changing and re-arranging of your inner man. God does the work through His Word and the Holy Spirit. He says so all over the Bible. In 1 Thessalonians He says:

> *Faithful is he that calleth you, who also will do it.* (1 Thess. 5:24 KJV)

God called you through this book, and maybe through other events in your life. He called you and He will perform a great work in you. The changes inside of you will be reflected in changed thoughts, habits, behaviors, and values.

But then, you'd have to read the Bible to see that and hear that, and know that. The Bible is not going to jump on your head and do a "mind meld" like Mr. Spock on Star Trek. You do have to put forth some effort friend.

"But that sounds boring and hard..." Which is harder? Living your whole life with nothing to show for it, without direction and purpose that you can see -- explaining to everyone you meet how it's someone else's fault that you have failed. God is putting a roadmap right in front of your eyes, right now. If you're too lazy to read the map, it's on you. God is so good that He even helps you to understand what you're reading. Like I said earlier, at first it feels like you're reading

Greek or Hebrew. (Actually you are because those languages are translated into English in our Bibles.) But if you want to know what you need to do, stick with it, and the Holy Spirit will begin to make it very clear. You'll even start to be rewarded with **revelation** -- God showing you something that no one has ever told you or taught you -- but you know it's the truth.

This lesson applies to Christians who have been Christians for 25 years too. If you haven't cracked you Bible in the last 20 years, don't expect a miracle. Don't expect abundance in your life. Don't expect the blessings that your Bible-reading, Bible-studying, praying, faith-filled neighbor gets. No, it's not about works, but you need to seek God to find Him. You need to demonstrate your faith by reading His Word daily -- even when nothing seems to be happening. You need to pray for someone besides yourself. Keep doing it, and I guarantee that something will happen. First of all, it will change you. Then it will change your circumstances.

Chapter Fifteen

Benefits of Walking the Way

A Prepared and Proven Path

There are advantages to walking in *The Way*. Anyone would admit that walking on a prepared and proven road is better than wandering through a dark forest with no clear path. In Isaiah 40:3-4, the prophet Isaiah predicts the coming of John the Baptist as a forerunner of Jesus Christ. John was described as:

> *A voice of one who cries: Prepare in the wilderness the way of the Lord [clear away the obstacles]; make straight and smooth in the desert a highway for our God!*

> *Every valley shall be lifted and filled up, and every mountain and hill shall*

*be made low; and the crooked and
uneven shall be made straight and
level, and the rough places a plain.*
(Isa. 40:3-4 AMP)

John the Baptist was a forerunner of Jesus. He came first to tell people that Jesus was coming soon. John taught the people to repent and be baptized. (To repent is to be sincerely sorry for sins and misdeeds. Repentance is to change one's mind and to turn to God.) He encouraged the people to prepare their hearts for the seeds of truth that Jesus would plant. John the Baptist even had the privilege of initiating the ministry of Jesus by baptizing Jesus.

Now Jesus has already walked the way and cleared the path for all who follow Him. He has led us to the highway of holiness in the wilderness of today's world. He will remove obstacles like addiction, low self-esteem, self-doubt, uncontrollable urges, perversion, hatred, unforgiveness, hypocrisy and lying -- just to name a few. These are habits and states of mind that we have often attempted to rid ourselves of without success. Through acceptance of Jesus Christ and the assistance of His Holy Spirit, these encumbrances can be eliminated from our path.

Every valley and low place can be lifted. Chronic depression and suicidal thoughts, moodiness, and hopelessness can be changed into a level road of peace and joy. All of the crooked places -- the diversions and distractions that so easily take us off the path, can be made straight, and the rough places in our lives can be eliminated.

There are many other advantages. I have experienced addiction, low self-esteem, rejection, hatred, unforgiveness and lying. But when I accepted Jesus, the guilt of all my wrongdoings and the desire to participate in unholy acts were washed away.

I was by no means a saint, brothers and sisters. I went through some of the same pitfalls you may have experienced. I searched under countless rocks and in many dark caves for salvation. I did not find the answers. Many times, I barely escaped with my life. I did not find help until I accepted Jesus Christ as my Lord and Savior. I now have peace and a purpose.

Holiness

The word "holiness" scares some people. But holiness is not a product of a lot of self-effort. It's not something that you have to do. Holiness comes with *The Way*. With a sincere effort to walk *The Way*, God will assist you. How? Isaiah 42 promises:

*And I will bring the blind by a way
that they know not; I will lead them in
paths that they have not known. I will
make darkness into light before them
and make uneven places into a plain.
These things I have determined to do
[for them]; and I will not leave them
forsaken.* (Isa. 42:16 AMP)

God will enlighten. To enlighten is to provide understanding of things that a person did
not understand before. Sometimes we walk in
darkness because we do not realize the full consequences of our actions. Even though we are
hurting ourselves and others, we are unaware
of the full consequences in the long term. God
promises to provide that floodlight of understanding for us and to make it easier to walk in
that knowledge. Then He promises that He will
not leave nor forsake us.

In Philippians 2:13 it reads:

*For it is God which worketh in you both
to will and to do of his good pleasure.*
(Phil. 2:13 KJV)

This scripture is saying that God works
within you after you accept Jesus as your Lord

and Savior. God works in you. How? You are changed on the inside. You find yourself wanting to do and enabled to do what pleases God. He does the work. You read and listen to His word. **He does the work**.

In Exodus God lets us know: ...*for I am the Lord that healeth thee*. (Exod. 15:26 KJV) God does the healing of physical illness, emotional illness, mental illness and soul sickness. Wherever the ailment is in your life, God does the healing. It is not your job, nor is it an expectation that you do the healing of yourself. God does the healing by His Word and His awesome supernatural power. All you have to do is believe in the one who God sent. The disciples asked Jesus "What shall we do, that we might work the works of God?" Jesus answered in John 6:

> *This is the work of God, that ye believe*
> *on him whom he hath sent.*
> (John 6:29b KJV)

Believe wholeheartedly in the life, death, burial and resurrection of the Lord Jesus Christ. Believe that He was and is the Son of God. Believe in the power of His blood shed on the cross.

Psalm 37 also promises light and righteousness.

> *Commit thy way unto the Lord; trust*
> *in him; and he shall bring it to pass.*
>
> *And he shall bring forth thy righteous-*
> *ness as the light, ...* (Ps. 37:5-6 KJV)

Just commit or give your way to the Lord God and trust in Him. He will bring to pass the fulfillment of your needs and your desires -- as long as they are in line with His will. He will also bring forth righteouness in you, and that righteousness will be like a light in you that others can see although they may not be able to verbalize it. They might say, "There's something different about you." or "You look different." or "You're not the same as you were last time I saw you." My point is: God does the work. He brings forth that righteousness from you. You don't have to strive for it.

Finally in Philippians 6 God says:

> *Being confident of this very thing, that*
> *he which hath begun a good work in*
> *you will perform it until the day of*
> *Jesus Christ.* (Phil. 6:6 KJV)

When you accepted Jesus Christ as your Lord and Savior earlier, God began a work in you -- a good work of right development. God's Word says that He will perform it. God will finish the work that He has started in you. Let God do the work. Your job is to believe.

There is a way that you can inadvertently wander out of *The Way*, and off the path. Mark 12 delivers a message from Jesus:

> *Jesus said to them, Is not this where you wander out of the way and go wrong, because you know neither the Scriptures nor the power of God?* (Mark 12:24 AMP)

Reading and meditating the Word of God, even a few verses each day, will provide strength and guidance on *The Way*. As you see the changes in yourself and your environment, you will be able to attest to the power of God.

To summarize, there are many benefits to walking *The Way*. This chapter only presents a few:

- A prepared and proven path
- Peace
- Holiness
- Understanding

- Righteousness
- Physical, emotional and mental healing
- Strength
- Guidance
- Completion of a good work inside of you

The greatest gift received is the forgiveness of our sins. This forgiveness frees us from guilt, shame, and condemnation. The scriptures below talk about our sins:

> *..Unto him [Jesus] that loved us, and washed us from our sins in his own blood,...* (Rev. 1:5b KJV) [Author's emphasis]

> *Who gave himself for our sins, that he [Jesus] might deliver us from this present evil world, according to the will of God and our Father.* (Gal. 1:4 KJV) [Author's emphasis]

> *Be it known unto you therefore, men and brethren, that through this man [Jesus] is preached unto you the forgiveness of sins: and by him all that believe are justified from all things, ...* (Acts 13:38-39a KJV) [Author's emphasis]

As far as the east is from the west, so far hath he removed our transgressions from us. (Ps. 103: 12 KJV

Jesus shed his blood to redeem mankind from sin and to offer forgiveness. A man or woman need only accept Jesus as their Lord and Savior. We are also justified, "pardoned and cleared from guilt". (Webster, Noah 2006) Our transgressions (sins and wrongdoings) are separated as far from us as the east is from the west.

There is therefore now no condemnation to them which are in Christ Jesus, who walk not after the flesh, but after the Spirit. (Rom. 8:1 KJV)

Chapter Sixteen

Closing Remarks

You have come a long way by completing this book. If you said the confession of the believer, you have stepped onto *The Way*. You have entered the path that leads to peace, joy, grace, and eternal life.

Since you've made a habit of reading daily, I encourage you to continue to read daily. Purchase a Bible or borrow one if need be. Read some of it every day. The words in the Bible are so powerful that just reading them changes you on the inside. That change is reflected in your thoughts and your behavior outside. It may seem like nothing is happening, but I assure you that each day you are growing in power -- from the inside out. You are growing.

Like a baby, you will move from the simple truths and understanding in the Word of God to understanding some of the secrets that God has reserved for those who love Him. You will grow deeper in faith. You will become wiser. Just knock on the door of God's Word. Ask God for wisdom. He promises that He will give wisdom to those who ask, and He won't remind you how dumb you have been in the past.

> *If any of you lack wisdom, let him ask of God, that giveth to all men liberally, and upbraideth not; and it shall be given him.* (James 1:5 KJV)

Upbraideth means to criticize severely; to find fault with; to scold. You remember how you have asked people questions in the past, even teachers. Some of them had to make you feel shame before giving an answer: "You don't know that? That is 4th-grade stuff." "You really ask some silly questions." "I can't believe you don't know that." But God gives you wisdom when you ask Him for it, and he doesn't scold you or sanction you for asking. He just gives you what you ask for. It is a process, which the Bible describes in Isaiah:

> *Whom shall he teach knowledge? and whom shall he make to understand doctrine? Them that are weaned from the milk, and drawn from the breasts.*

> *For precept must be upon precept, pre-*
> *cept upon precept; line upon line, line*
> *upon line; here a little and there a little.*
> (Isa .28:9-10 KJV)

A **precept**, according to *Merriam-Webster's Collegiate Dictionary* (2006) is "a command or principle especially as a general rule of action". Strong's Concordance (Strong, J. *The New Strong's Exhaustive Concordance of the Bible*. Comfort Print Edition. Nashville, TN: Thomas Nelson Publishers, 1995) defines precept as "an injunction or command". Precepts provide guidelines or signposts along *The Way*. You find these signposts in the Word of God or in a sermon, or in a book like this one. As you hear and read them, you begin to build your Christian character. You begin to grow as a Christian. Each line of God's Word is a building block for you. Here a little. There a little. As you put the pieces together, by the guidance of God's Holy Spirit, you develop into a mature Christian man or woman. You become stable and confident in walking *The Way*. You can even share with others who are lost.

One precept that I want to discuss is crucial to your growth and your survival in *The Way*. It is found in Proverbs 18:

> *Death and life are in the power of the tongue: and they that love it shall eat the fruit thereof.* (Prov. 18:21 KJV)

The Amplified version reads:

> *Death and life are in the power of the tongue, and they who indulge in it shall eat the fruit of it [for death or life].* (Prov. 18:21 AMP)

The Message Bible interprets it this way:

> *Words kill, words give life; they're either poison or fruit -- you choose.* (Prov. 18:21 The Message)

The tongue is a powerful instrument. It can be used as a weapon against yourself and against others -- sometimes unknowingly. Examples: "She makes me sick." "I never get what I need." "I guess I'll be poor forever." "No one is going to hire me." "I wish that guy would just drop dead and stay out of my life." "Boy, you will never amount to anything." [said to a child]

By making such statements, you are bringing sickness upon yourself. You are decreeing that you don't and will not get what you need. You are declaring poverty in your life and ruining your chances of getting a job. You are calling for a person to die or destroying a child's life by pronouncing that he will never be successful.

These unguarded remarks and exclamations, spoken when angry or discouraged, can reset the course of your life or the life of someone else. Watch your mouth! You can be on the road to success and speak one careless phrase against yourself that messes it all up. Words are that powerful. Learn to speak what God speaks in His Word. Bless people instead of cursing them with profanity and bad predictions. You must control your mouth. **THAT IS A POWERFUL PRECEPT.**

It may not be easy at first. Whenever you slip and say the wrong thing about yourself or someone else, immediately say: "I cancel that statement in the Name of Jesus. Forgive me Lord."

Pray daily. It does not have to be fancy, or loud, or profound. Just talk to God like you talk to a trusted friend -- minus any profanity, of course. Thank Him for your salvation and all that He has done for you, and all that He is still doing in your life. You can pray for yourself, but don't forget to pray for others as well. Your words carry power.

To those of you who did not say the confession for salvation, I ask you to review this book and reconsider your decision. You've tried many things that did not work. Why not try Jesus? He loves you, and He wants to deliver you from the prison in which you have placed yourself. Jesus is the key. Trust Him.

Father God, I pray that everyone who reads this book in its entirety, or even partially is touched by Your Word therein. I pray that each one is drawn to salvation with a desire to walk in *The Way* that You have provided for us. I decree that in confessing Jesus Christ as Lord and Savior, each one is freed from sin and delivered from the snares of the enemy. In the mighty name of Jesus, I pray. Amen.

References

Merriam-Webster's Collegiate Dictionary. Eleventh Edition. Springfield, MA: Merriam-Webster, 2006.

NIV/The Message Parallel Study Bible. Grand Rapids, MI: Zondervan, 2008.

Strong, James. *The New Strong's Exhaustive Concordance of the Bible.* Comfort Print Edition. Nashville, TN: Thomas Nelson Publishers, 1995.

The Amplified Bible. LaHabra, CA: Zondervan Corporation and the Lockman Foundation, 1987.

The Holy Bible (Authorized King James Version). Nashville, TN: Holman Bible Publishers, 1998.

The Webster International Dictionary. London, England: G. & C. Merriam Company, 1909.

Webster, Noah. *American Dictionary of the English Language*. First Edition of 1828. San Francisco, CA: Foundation for American Christian Education, 2006.

Other Books by
Jannah Mitchell

Al-Uqdah, Jannah. *Teaching Our Babies to Read: A Guide for African-American Parents.* Al-Uqdah Enterprises, Chicago, IL (1993)

Like a Tree Planted, Xulon Press, 2008